# Bent But Not Broken

Learning to love yourself
and discover your worth
over the next **30-days**

# Ashley Davis

# Bent But Not Broken

Learning to love yourself
and discover your worth
over the next **30-days**

## Ashley Davis

Printed in the United States of America by
T&J Publishers (Atlanta, GA.)
www.TandJPublishers.com



Cover Design by Timothy Flemming, Jr.
(T&J Publishers)
Book Format/Layout by Timothy Flemming, Jr.

ISBN: 978-1-7360003-0-4

To contact the author, go to:

AshleyDavis.asd@gmail.com
www.AshleyShantel.com
Facebook: Ashley Davis
Instagram: Ashleyd_Speaks
Twitter: AshleyD_Speaks

# DEDICATION

I would like to dedicate this book to both my daughters, Aniya Underwood and Kyndel Davis. Being a mother is not easy; it makes you look at yourself in the mirror and face your flaws. Being a mother is challenging because I strive to make sure that neither of you make the same mistakes that I made. I see much of myself in both of you, and it's like a dream.

It is a blessing to watch you both grow into beautiful young ladies. You have helped me to grow up, to desire more out of life, and to live better. Of course, I'm not perfect, but everyday on this earth is another opportunity for me to better myself.

The only thing I can say to you is do great, be yourselves, love yourselves, and always put God first.

# ACKNOWLEDGMENTS

To my daughters, Kyndel and Aniya, thank you for encouraging me to go after my dreams. You are my heartbeats, and my goal is to continue to set a good example for you. I love you both.

I would like to thank my mother, Artis Lary, for demonstrating what it takes to be responsible in life and a hard worker. You have always supported my decisions both good and bad. Thanks for being my backbone when I didn't have one. I love you.

I would like to thank my step dad, Emmett Lary, for showing me tough love and helping me to focus on my needs and not just my wants. I love you.

I would like to thank Eric Bronner for encouraging me to never get complacent in life, and to always add to what I have. I love you.

To my family and friends, thank you for all of the love and support you have shown me.

Thank you Lamar with Lundizign for my nice photos.

To Stacey Cook-Davis, thank you for being a listening ear, and thank you for your encouraging words. I love you.

Lastly, thank you for my mentor, Niya Matthews. You have been such a blessing to me. You helped me to bring my vision to life. Thank you for your encouraging words, direction, and understanding.

This book is also dedicated to all of those who are on the journey towards true life, love, great relationships, and self-love. I wrote this book just for you to answer the questions many of you may have. I know you are going to find what you are looking for and experience God's best for your life. May God continue to bless each of you.

# Table of Contents

# Day 1

## I LOVE EVERYTHING
## ABOUT MY BODY

*I praise you because I am fearfully and wonderfully made;*
*your works are wonderful; I know that full well.*
—Psalm 139:14

+ I will spend more time looking in the mirror and admiring my body just the way that it is.

+ I will think positive thoughts about my body and go throughout my day with a positive attitude.

Appreciating your physical body is important. When you love the body you have, you will develop a level of self-esteem and confidence that will prevent you from becoming intimidated by others. You won't feel intimidated by how other people look, and you won't be vulnerable to manipulative people who try to tear you down mentally because of your looks. This world would be a boring place if everyone looked the same. God created us in his image, and everything that he created was made perfect, so if you lack confidence in your image then take the necessary steps to change the way you look: lose weight, walk, jog, tone, and eat healthier meals.

To change the way your body looks, you must first change the way you think. You won't get results overnight, which may be frustrating, but you must keep in mind how exciting it will be once you get the body you want, when all of your hard work has paid off. Just make sure that your goal of weight loss is for yourself and not for someone else. Ignore body-shaming statements thrown at you from people who want to make you feel bad due to their insecurities. Focus instead on developing the best body you can for yourself; doing so will make this endeavour special.

I battled with low self-esteem due to not having the flattest tummy and the biggest bottom. I exercised and ate healthily; however, it didn't seem like I was getting the results that I wanted. Recently, I paid money to have a Brazilian Butt Lift. I was very excited about having that procedure and assumed that my life would be a lot better after having the procedure. But four days before the surgery, I cancelled my appointment and requested a refund. The Coronavirus was gaining national attention due to its rapid spreading, which made my family fearful about me having the procedure. I felt like that was God pumping my brakes—preventing me from having the procedure. Perhaps he was allowing me to save my money due to the pandemic, knowing what challenges lied ahead. Afterwards, I began working out and eating healthy. Not only did I feel great, but I began to look great also. I had to trust the process of transformation. And remember: The right people will love you regardless of how you look, and they will focus on your value as a human being rather than devalue you because of your physical image.

> "My smile is my favorite part of my body; I think a smile can make your whole body. I want women to know that it's okay to be whatever size you are and be beautiful inside and out."
>
> —Serena Williams

## Notes

1.) Has there ever been a time when you were not confident with your physical appearance?

2.) What steps did you take to get the figure/look that you wanted?

3.) Were you surrounded by people that complimented you on the way you look? Who were they?

4.) How did you encourage yourself?

_______________________________________

_______________________________________

_______________________________________

_______________________________________

_______________________________________

_______________________________________

_______________________________________

_______________________________________

_______________________________________

_______________________________________

# Day 2

## LOVING UNCONDITIONALLY

*And so, we know and rely on the love God has for us. God is love, whoever lives in love lives in God, and God is them.*
—1 John 4:16

• I will not criticize my partner's flaws, but I will build him up and lift him up with my words.

• I will make my mate feel loved and happy without expecting anything in return.

To love unconditionally can be hard because we are only humans. That means we have flaws, shortcomings, weaknesses, and problems of our own to deal with. We find our love being tested by our partners when they are out of character, say mean things to us, violate our trust, irritate us, and act in complicated ways. And to make matters worse, no one has the same upbringing, background, beliefs, spiritual perspective, and temperament, and these differences play a major role in the way we interact and communicate with one another. Due to these differences in perspective, there are times when, for the sake of peace, we choose to be silent and withhold our opinions. There are times when we have to ignore the flaws of our partners so that we can focus on and keep at the forefront of our minds the things we love about them—the things that caused us to fall in-love with them from the beginning.

Once you accept a person for who they are, flaws and all, you'll learn how to communicate with them without triggering them and causing friction; you'll learn how to avoid toxic emotions like disappointment and resentment. For example, if a person was not brought up in a household where love and affection were shown, you cannot expect a strong display of love and affection from them. You just know that's not their strong point. They might show love in different ways: buying gifts, taking you out on dates, and more. Their love-language may be different. Most people don't have the same love language. But knowing these things about your partner—knowing their love-language—allows you to be more patient and understanding towards them so that you can deal with them more effectively. Patience is a virtue, and love is often demonstrated by being sensitive and understanding of another person's needs, flaws, and challenges. The more you understand why a person is the way they are, the less angry you become with them. Like the Bible says, "Wisdom is the principal thing; therefore, *get* wisdom and in *all thy getting, get understanding*" (Proverbs 4:7).

My love and patience for other people have certainly been tested. At times, people have treated me in ways that made me question myself; I would wonder if I did something wrong to deserve the reactions they gave me. I would do my best to empathize with them, to see things through their eyes and understand where they were coming from. Practicing empathy and carefully studying and observing the other people in my life allowed me to develop a greater understanding of them. This understanding enabled me to communicate with them better and avoid hitting certain triggers that would elicit a negative reaction out of them. Gaining an understanding of these individuals has even made it easier for me to forgive them when they're wrong, knowing why they did what they did. Of course, I'm not foolish enough to put myself in the same position to get hurt, but through understanding, forgiveness came easier. And forgiveness is a must. Why? Because God forgave us. Furthermore, God places certain people in our lives for a reason. Not everyone God sends your way is going to agree with you and do things the same way as you. That doesn't mean they aren't supposed to be in your life; on the contrary, they may be just what you need. Don't put a period where God placed a comma. Don't end a relationship just because of a few differences. Learn to recognize and even value these differences; they help you to grow and expand in your thinking and understanding. So pray, meditate, and ask God to give you a love for other people. Ask God to teach you how to love others the way He loves them, view others the way He views them, and treat them the way you would want to be treated.

> "Love has nothing to do with what you are expecting to get, only with what you are expecting to give."
> —Katherine Hepburn

## Notes

1.) Has your love for someone ever encountered a challenge?

2.) How did you handle that situation?

3.) When upset, do you become distant towards others, or do you focus on finding solutions to the things that upset you?

_______________________________________________

_______________________________________________

_______________________________________________

_______________________________________________

# Day 3

## WHY YOUR LOVE
## NEEDS BOUNDARIES

*For God is not the author of confusion; He's the author of peace.*
—1 CORINTHIANS 14:33

+ I will pray before I over-think things and make a mess of my life.

+ I will protect my peace.

Creating boundaries is necessary to protect our hearts. If we do not set boundaries, then we will fail to teach other people how to treat us, and they will continue to cross the line regarding us. Boundaries help us create balance in our lives. In relationships, boundaries should be established upfront without compromising. We must let our mates know what we will and will not accept. Once we let our guards down and compromise on our standards, we will allow others to manipulate our thoughts and overstep their boundaries. Once the manipulation starts, the other person will act as if they know what's best for you, and as if you can't think and do for yourself; this will negatively affect your self-esteem. Never allow another person to play with your emotions and make you feel as if you can't think and do for yourself.

Love usually causes us to overlook a lot of things about our partners and loved-ones, that is until they continue to cross certain lines. When this happens, we begin to feel overwhelmed, like we're about to go into Cardiac Arrest. Cardiac Arrest is caused by putting intense pressure on the heart; such happens when trying to keep peace in a relationship that you are unhappy within. We put up with things we shouldn't put up with due to the fear of losing the relationship. That's not love. That's a toxic situation that will erode your health and land you in a hospital…or a morgue.

When a person is truly into you, they will do what it takes to keep a smile on your face; they will respect your boundaries and seek to align themselves with your standards. Unfortunately, in relationships, you will get tested, and if you don't put an end to negative habits early on, things will get worse; it will get harder and harder to break those habits as time progresses. The line of communication should be clear. No party involved in the relationship should feel afraid to speak his or her mind. Both individuals will respect each other's opinions, feelings, and beliefs. Both individuals will seek to honor each other and embrace one another's differences. That is why you must be emotionally mature before entering into a relationship such as a marriage. You don't want to be "unequally yoked" with someone who is selfish, self-centered, mentally and emotionally immature, thinking that everything revolves around them alone. Being in this type of relationship will allow the devil to play on your heart and mind and emotions. You can't blame God for being in that type of relationship; He's not forcing you to remain there. He's not the one producing fear and confusion inside of you either; He's a God of peace, and His blessings are designed to enhance your life, not drain you. The person God sends you will add to your life, not take away from it. God's partner for you will respect who you are, not try to take advantage of you.

I have been in a relationship where I failed to set boundaries. These situations only placed more and more stress, grief, and sadness in my life; they only left me feeling drained and depressed. At times, I was afraid to speak my mind. The fear of being alone controlled me. I allowed myself to be manipulated and controlled. I would even try to justify my situation by telling myself, "No one is perfect, and you are going to have to deal with something you won't like." Still, that didn't help or change anything. At times, after communicating with the controlling partner, I'd feel worse than before. I would get blamed for everything going wrong and be made to feel ashamed. I wouldn't stand up for myself. I never wanted to perceive other people in a negative light, so I'd try to think the best of them and give them the benefit of the doubt. But I was just fooling myself. I was allowing myself to be manipulated and taken advantage of. It took me a while to discover that this wasn't love; that love actually possesses boundaries, and it is built on respect. None of that is God's will. Set boundaries—you'll feel better.

## NOTES

1.) What boundaries have you set in your relationship?

2.) Have you ever been manipulated?

3.) What boundaries will you set in your current or next relationship?

___________________________________________

___________________________________________

___________________________________________

___________________________________________

___________________________________________

___________________________________________

# Day 4

## LOVING THEIR POTENTIAL

*Do everything in love.*
—1 Corinthians 16:14

+ I will accept people where they are in their lives.

+ I will not compare myself to others.

Sometimes, it's easier to fall in love with an idea than it is a real person. We can fool ourselves in relationships by focusing more on what we hope our partners will become than who and what they are. We blind ourselves to their true character. When our partner's treat us with kindness, we tend to overlook the bad things they do to us. We often succumb to their charms and forget about the way they make us feel after they get what they want from us. Some of us may be in relationships with partners who display mood swings, quickly going from happy to sad, from calm to explosive, nice and considerate to disrespectful and mean seemingly at a drop of a dime. They start out valuing us and then later place other people and things in front of us.

Through denial, we blindfold ourselves in relationships to avoid seeing the true person standing before us. We don't want to acknowledge the truth about them and face the pain and disappointment. It hurts—it really hurts—to fall in love with someone whose character you can't stand. You feel bad about falling for such a person. Furthermore, the longer you stay with them, the harder it gets to pull away from them. But remember: You cannot continuously make excuses for an adult who knows right from wrong. By excusing their behaviors and making excuses for them, you're handicapping them and preventing them from growing up.

God gave us all the gift of intuition. If, at any point in time, you feel as if there is something that is not right, take heed to that feeling; it could be the Holy Spirit guiding you, steering you away from a person or situation. You most certainly need divine guidance when it comes to the area of relationships because you don't know what's in a person's heart; you don't know what the other person is like behind closed doors, but God knows. God sees what you don't see.

Don't fall in love with an idea, with an image. Don't fall in love with a fantasy. Don't become fixated on an idea of how things should be while ignoring how they are. Don't jump into a relationship thinking you're going to "fix" or change someone into the ideal mate. That's a mistake. Come out of the fantasy world and step back into the real world, the world that currently exists, not the world you envision. Keep your eyes open and be vigilant. Look for signs and red flags. As you get closer to obtaining the ring, skeletons will begin to come out of the closet, and true attitudes will start to be exposed. Your love will then be tested, and you'll be forced to ask yourself an important question: "Is this something I want to live with for the rest of my life?" Remember, you can't change another person; you can only work on yourself so that you can become a better person, a better version of yourself. You can only make yourself easier to love. So decide what you want to live with and who you want to be in life. Yes, believe in the other person's ability to change and pray for them, hope for it, but do so while making wise decisions for yourself.

## NOTES

1.) Have you ever fallen in love with someone's potential? If so, how did it make you feel?

2.) What steps did you take to correct the problems that you and your partner faced?

3.) Did communication help?

# Day 5

## SOUL-TIES

*But I say, walk by the Spirit, and you will*
*not gratify the desires of the flesh.*
—Galatians 5:16

♦ I will pray and ask God to guide my thoughts and reactions.

♦ Lord, strengthen me in my weakest moments.

Soul-ties happen in every sexually intimate relationship. Ideally, two people should become "one" and then draw closer to God together, but this isn't always the case; in fact, this is rarely the case. Many people misuse sex and create soul-ties that draw them away from God; and in many of these cases, these couples end up drifting apart once the excitement of the relationship wears off. Afterwards, the move on to establish soul-ties with other people.

Many of us have developed strong soul-ties with other partners. And you know you have a soul-tie because even after the relationship has come to an end and you have pulled away from that person, something keeps you going back to them; you can't seem to break free from them and move on with your life. That's a sign of a soul-tie. You keep smelling your mate's cologne or perfume while out in public, and you keep daydreaming about them and obsessing over them, even to the point of stalking them. Also, you find yourself acting out of character. You've centered your life around this person even though the two of you are incompatible and can hardly get along.

A soul-tie is a spiritual phenomenon; the only way to break one is through prayer. You must ask God to remove the soul-ties that are in your life, which you've established through sexual contact with others, whether they be "friends with benefits," former lovers, one-night-stands, or *whoever.*

There is a difference between a soul-mate and a soul-tie. You become soul-mates with another person when the two of you are mutually and equally interested in each other in every way, and not just in the bedroom. When dealing with a soul-mate, it isn't one person doing all of the work and all of the pursuing; both are mentally, emotionally, spiritually, and physically invested in the relationship.

With a soul-tie, you're still attached to a sexual partner or partners even after the relationship or relationships have ended. Why? Because your souls, during sex, become intertwined. Your emotions are still attached to that person because your spirit is still attached to them. That is why it is important to wait until marriage before having sex and to know who you're marrying before walking down the aisle. It's important to pray and ask God to lead you to the right person so that you won't become attached to the wrong person. You must guard your heart and pay close attention to certain red flags early so that you can avoid serious heartbreak.

> "I think you have different SOUL-MATES throughout your life, that your soul needs different THINGS at different TIMES."
>
> —KIM KARDASHIAN

## NOTES

1.) Have you ever experienced having a soul-tie?

2.) How did you discover that you were dealing with a soul-tie?

3.) How did you get delivered from that soul-tie?

_______________________________________________

_______________________________________________

_______________________________________________

_______________________________________________

_______________________________________________

_______________________________________________

_______________________________________________

_______________________________________________

_______________________________________________

_______________________________________________

# Day 6

## REJECTION

*Be alert and of sober mind. Your enemy the devil prowls around like a roaring lion looking for someone to devour.*
—1 Peter 5:8

+ I will take time to process what has happened.

+ I will focus on the lesson, how to grow and move forward.

Rejection does not feel good. Sometimes, the pain of rejection can feel as though it will never end. Behind rejection can follow feelings of paranoia, as if everyone knows our business. If you are not in tune with your feelings and haven't given yourself time to heal, rejection will lead to depression. Our actions can cause others to react towards us with rejection. Sadly, when others respond to us with rejection, this tends to lead us into darker pits. For example, to cope with the pain of rejection, we isolate ourselves and choose to be alone. Now, it's fine to take some time to yourself to heal, to give yourself over to meditation and prayer so that you can refocus and regain the strength to move forward with your life. But remaining isolated so that you can lick your wounds is dangerous and destructive. Get around people who love and value you. Also, be careful about seeking advice from family and friends; it can be good at times to do so, but there's the possibility of them giving you bad or confusing advice or even attempting to control how you act. They may try to make you respond the way they would as opposed to the way God wants you to respond to the situation. And they truly do love you. Their emotions are tied up into you and your well-being.

But the wisest thing you can do is take some time and be still so that you can hear from God and receive clear and precise instructions from Him regarding the matter.

When rejected, don't attempt to numb your pain; instead, confront it. Seeking a counselor is greatly beneficial because you will be confiding in someone who is not biased towards you and your situation. They don't know you, so they will be impartial and subjective in the situation and tell you what you need to hear without any strings attached. They will teach you how to process the rejection without passing judgment on yourself and others.

Here's another good piece of advice: Do not go around your ex after rejection because doing so can rekindle old feelings and put you in a precarious position. If you must do so, block them—block their calls, don't respond to their texts and emails. Why? Because you're still weak to them. Give yourself time to heal and gain strength.

Rejection can play on our thoughts. The situation that led to the rejection tends to stay on our mind's day in and day out. However, it is important to remember that the person who rejected you is not God. Ask yourself why their rejection stings so much? What is it about them that makes them so special they have the right to consume your every thought? Truthfully, they're not that special. Furthermore, you had a life before them and "this too shall pass." Go on and live with or without them. Do other things to fill your time and keep yourself busy, such as taking up a hobby you've always wanted. Focus on treating yourself and doing things that make you happy. In due time, the pain will go away.

My experience with rejection hit me hard. I figured I was on my way down the aisle, but things took a different turn, and I had to walk away from the relationship. I was tired of being disrespected. However, even though I thought I was ready to end things, I still felt in my heart that I shouldn't. Never make rash decisions and end a relationship hastily or react on emotions without considering all aspects of what's going on. After all, once you officially end the relationship, the other person may move on with their life. At the time, I did consider whether or not it was a wise decision to be patient and work things out. I didn't think about whether I was ready to see them with someone else. I didn't think about what my life would even look like moving forward. I just broke up with my ex. When my ex didn't respond to the break-up the way that I hoped he would, it left me in a low place. I was sad for quite some time. I even turned to psychics on YouTube, trying to gain insight on what they were feeling and how things would play out.

I believed in God, and I had faith, but when I was in a sunken place, praying for God to bring him back to me, he seemed to get further away from me. I sought advice from family and friends, which left me even more confused. Some advised me to move on, and others tried to give me tips on how to win him back that sounded ridiculous. I was in love, so letting go was not easy for me. I knew that "shacking" was wrong, but I figured that being the first person your significant other sees when they wake-up and the last person they see before going to be was special. And they are. Those moments shouldn't be taken for granted because not everyone that goes to sleep gets to wake up in the morning to behold a brand new day, and not everyone that wakes up actually makes it through the day. I eventually overcame my pain by praying consistently, finding hobbies, focusing on myself and the kids, starting my own business, and doing productive things to get to a new level in my life. Sometimes God will remove people from our lives, especially after we've inadvertently made them a god. God is a jealous God, and we are not to put anyone or anything before Him.

As time progressed, God has revealed things to me that helped me to understand why that separation needed to happen. Our relationship wasn't built on the right foundation and with the right material. You can work on building your relationship, but if it's not built on the right foundation and with the right material, it will fall apart.  A relationship falling apart is not always a bad thing. It takes trial, tests, circumstances, and sometimes, distance, to help you realize what you need in life and even to help you get it right the next time around. Your vision will be clearer once the pain goes away, as mine did.

## Notes

1.) Why did you feel rejected?

2.) How did you overcome the pain of rejection?

3.) Did you abandon your faith in God due to the rejection?

4.) If you were to experience rejection again, how would you deal with it and cope with your emotions?

________________________________________________

________________________________________________

________________________________________________

________________________________________________

________________________________________________

________________________________________________

# Day 7

## WHY DO I KEEP GOING
## BACK TO HIM/HER?

*The Lord is close to the brokenhearted and
saves those who are crushed in spirit.*
—Psalm 34:18

+ I will overcome my fear of being alone.

+ I will not lower my standards for anyone.

Have you ever been in love with someone? If so, then you know the feeling. You know that "butterflies in the stomach" feeling, the feeling of obsession. You also know it can be difficult, even seemingly impossible to let that person go. I mean, there you are, ready to walk away from the relationship, and then you receive a text from them, and suddenly, all of those feelings of attraction come flooding through you, and you're hooked once again. You can't help yourself. Your body lights up like a Christmas tree. You begin to think about the fun times the two of you shared. You think about how they smelled, the cologne they wore, the intimate moments you created together, the many nights filled with pillow talk, even the times when the two of you went through tough moments and were there for one another. You think about the many times you were excited to share with them some good news. You think about the dates you had, not thinking about the incompatibility issues between the two of you.

When you feel tempted to return to your ex, I want you to pause for a moment and remember the reason or reasons you left them in the first place. Remember about how they made you feel during disagreements. Think about the disrespect, the abuse, the manipulation, the control. And afterwards, if you have to, thank yourself for getting out of the relationship when you did and forgive yourself for staying in it longer than you should have. Think about the *what* and *why* behind your decision to leave. Once you figure those two things out, you'll find it easier to move on with your life, regret-free. Look yourself in the mirror each day and remind yourself that you are worthy and deserving of better. Love yourself enough to realize that you are the answer to someone else's prayers and that a better situation is coming your way.

In the moments when you are still, God is working on your behalf. He is preparing for you the right person. Until then, work on becoming a better you. Allow yourself time to heal, and to work on the triggers in your life that cause you to act out of character. Focus on improving your temperament. Suddenly, you will look up and, just like that, you will attract the right person based on the new person that you have become.

> "Lots of people want to ride with you in the limo, but you need someone who will help you catch the bus."
>
> —Oprah Winfrey

## Notes

1.) What is so special about the person you keep returning to?

2.) What is it about this person that makes you weak?

3.) Does this person have the same amount of interest in you?

4.) Is a relationship with this person worth fighting for?

5.) Did you self-reflect before walking away from this person?

# Day 8

## AM I A PROVERBS 31 WOMAN?

*She will do him good and not evil all the days of her life.*
—Proverbs 31:12

+ I do not have to be a perfect woman to be a well-loved woman.

+ I have good morals and integrity.

As women, most of us strive to be a Proverbs 31 woman. To accomplish this goal, it takes prayer. Furthermore, we must learn to put God first. Being a virtuous woman is not easy. It takes time to become this type of woman. To become women of virtue, we must develop strength, wisdom, integrity, discipline, dignity, faithfulness, and temperance. We must learn to watch our tongues and temper our words. Challenges will arise, but we must keep our peace and maintain the right perspective in the situation.

Behaviors are learned. If we have developed habits and personality traits that are in conflict with the person we are trying to become, this can be discouraging. But we can become the person we envision ourselves to be. It's possible. We just have to realize that change doesn't happen overnight; it takes time and requires growth. We change little by little, grow little by little. And keep in mind that change is growth. As we become conscious of each little habit and make the small changes needed to correct these things, we are growing into the person we want to be.

If you are working on self-improvement, do it for yourself; don't do it for the purpose of gaining the approval of a man or woman. You will fall short and make mistakes along the way, but that doesn't mean you've failed. That is a part of the process of change and growth, so don't give up. Keep pushing, and start each day by affirming yourself with these words: "I have another chance to work on myself and my weaknesses." Tests will come, and when they do, take what you have learned and apply it. Nothing can happen without God's permission, and He will not put more on you than you can bear.

I am a work in progress. I am very flawed, but I take each day as a new opportunity to become a better me. Every day, I am slowly becoming that Proverbs 31 woman. Every day, I am discovering little things I need to change, and I am working on changing them. Each day that passes, I am growing. It's time for you to become the person you were meant to become also.

"Every woman is virtuous in her own way; it's all in what her mate is looking for."

—Ashley Davis

## Notes

1.) Have you ever asked God to make you a virtuous woman?

2.) Have you observed any growth and maturity in your life?

3.) What steps did you take to improve upon yourself?

__________________________________________________

__________________________________________________

__________________________________________________

# Day 9

## ARE THEY LOSING INTEREST?

*He gives strength to the weary and*
*increases the power of the weak.*
—Isaiah 40:29

+ I will practice self-love and do things that make me happy.

+ I will accept God's will for my life.

Depending on where you are in a relationship, it may seem like your mate is losing interest in you. Again, we've all been gifted with intuition, which enables us to sense when something isn't quite right. At times, we can sense when something is off with our partners and when our relationships are out of balance. During moments like these, we tend to reflect on our relationships, as we should. One thing that helps during these moments is pulling out a pen and piece of paper and writing your observations down. Examine the "then" and the "now" state of affairs in the relationship. Examine closely what may be the causes of the observable changes. Take note of any changes that may have occurred within yourself and your partner. For example, have you or your partner developed any insecurities, or has there been a change in your goals and values as individuals? Changes such as these can cause an unbalance in the relationship and lead to one partner losing interest in the other.

When dealing with an imbalance in your relationship, I like to use the analogy of a computer. Computers are controlled by software. That software tells the computer how to behave. In relationships, we all have software that we come downloaded with (beliefs, coping mechanisms, ideals, expectations, and more), and sometimes we may need to reprogram and even reboot the relationship. We may need to re-examine our way of doing things and handling situations and realize that what may have worked before may not work now. We may need to go back and look at our software and see if it is effective. Most importantly, we need to be humble enough to admit when we need to make changes within to improve ourselves, and then take the necessary steps to make those changes. If things don't begin to improve in the relationship at that point after you've made the changes and corrections within yourself that need to be made, then it's not a problem with you, it's a problem with your partner. You may need to sit down with them and have a heart-to-heart and ask them about their feelings and expectations.

You can tell when things are out of balance. Little things you used to do together, you no longer do. For example, your relationship is in trouble when you and your partner no longer go out on dates, when the two of you don't go anywhere together anymore if you or your partner is always annoyed when one of you try to have a conversation, and when you begin to avoid one another. These are serious red flags. If your partner doesn't want you to touch them, they no longer care about these things that interest you, and arguments are escalating, it's time to seriously seek the Lord in prayer and seek a good relationship counselor. Don't just assume things are going to get better on their own, because they're not.

I've been in that situation. I was in a relationship with a partner who seemed to be losing interest in our relationship. I tried everything in my power to make things work. There were times when I felt like I was giving 80% while he was only giving 20%. But I kept fighting. I believed that anything worth having is worth fighting for and that the fight wouldn't be easy. At times, it looked like my prayers were paying off, and at other times, I felt as if God was telling me to let it go and walk away. When encountering this situation, confusion sets in. We know God is not the author of confusion, so I realized that when confused, I needed to pull away momentarily in order to better hear from God and gain clarity, which is what I did. When I did this, peace flooded my soul, and I discovered that some of what I was feeling were my selfish nature telling me to hold on to something as if my life depended on it. That's not God's will. What the Lord puts together, no man can tear apart. When God is behind something, it flows smoothly like oil. You don't have to "make" or "force" things to happen—make or force someone to stay in your life and value you. That person will have the grace to love you. Yes, you will always need to work on yourself to improve who you are, but that person will have the grace to walk with you through the journey. So here's my advice to you: get into a quiet place with God where you can hear Him speak to you, and learn to "be still and know" that He is God. Stop stressing and worrying and let Him guide you through this season. If they stay, good; if not, then God has something better. Either way, know that you are enough.

## Notes

1.) Have you ever felt unwanted in a relationship?

2.) What steps did you take to fix your relationship?

________________________________________________

________________________________________________

________________________________________________

________________________________________________

# DO I SACRIFICE MY HAPPINESS
# FOR MY FAMILY?

*The Lord is my strength and my shield; my heart*
*trusts in him, and he helps me. My heart leaps*
*for joy, and with my song I praise him.*
—PSALM 28:7

- I will not share my relationship issues with my family and friends.

- My mate's responsibility is to focus on my happiness, not my family and friends' happiness.

Don't feel bad about loving someone who makes you happy, even if they're viewed differently by others. Your family and friends can only see the surface of your mate, but you have gotten to know them much deeper than that; you know their soul. Many people like to criticize our choices in life and try to impose their preferences and desires on us; they want our relationships to look like something they had in mind. Get ready for it—there will be some people who will be happy for you when you announce your chosen mate, and there will be some who will be critical. There will be some people who will try to compare your relationship to theirs despite the fact that theirs is full of problems. Rather than acknowledging that there are no perfect people and no perfect relationships, they'll try to hold yours to a standard they can't even obtain.

Some parents tend to feel entitled to all of their children's attention and feel neglected and even betrayed when someone else comes into their children's lives. But when you find yourself in a new place in life, living in a new season, you must embrace the changes that come with it. You have to put boundaries around your relationship to protect it even from family members. What this means is you may have to limit the amount of time you spend on the phone. You will have to compromise with your partner when it comes to whose house you're going to spend the holidays at. Your family can't hog all of your time and attention.

Let me warn you now: there will be those friends and family members who'll come along and accuse you of putting your partner before them; they'll even say mean things about your partner in order to change your perspective of them. That's being selfish. They're not thinking about your happiness and your needs.

There were times when I've sought advice from family and friends only for them to try to steer me in a direction that favored their personal self-interests. At times, they would side with me in matters, as you'd expect, as opposed to being objective. That is why I've learned that, regarding certain matters, it's best not to seek counsel from friends and family. Rely on your intuition instead and seek an objective party such as a counselor. Too many opinions from family and friends can have a negative impact on your home and cause unnecessary problems.

Yes, trials and tribulations will arise in your relationship; that is common. But communication is the key to working through these things. If you walk away from your relationship just to make certain people happy, you will end up miserable in the long run, and sadly, those same people you tried to please will go on with their personal lives despite your unhappiness. Have the strength and courage to stand up for the partner you've chosen and teach your family and friends to respect your decision.

## Notes

1.) Do you try to make your family and friends happy?

2.) Does your family and friends' opinions play a role in your decisions regarding your relationship?

3.) What other steps can you take besides involving family and friends when in need of help in your relationship?

__________________________________________

__________________________________________

__________________________________________

__________________________________________

__________________________________________

__________________________________________

__________________________________________

__________________________________________

__________________________________________

__________________________________________

# Day 11

## OVERCOMING BITTERNESS

*Then Peter came to Jesus and asked, "Lord, how many times shall I forgive my brother or sister who sins against me? Up to seven times? Jesus answered, "I tell you not seven times, but seventy-seven times.*
—Matthew 18:21–22

+ I will give 100% in my relationship, so that should it end, I will have no regrets.

+ I will not base my life around another person. I will focus on and live my life also.

Getting over a breakup can be hard; it can leave you in a sunken place. The hurt from a breakup can cause you to blame yourself for the erosion of the relationship as if most or even everything that happened was your fault. Feeling this way can cause a sense of bitterness. Remember, it is normal to be sad, but it is not normal to be bitter behind a breakup. There is a thin line between sadness and bitterness, so you must encourage yourself during these times of heartbreak. Realize that God has a bright destiny for your life and that breakup isn't the end of your life.

Whenever God removes someone from your life, He will replace them with someone better. If the relationship came to an end, chances are it wasn't right for you or built on the right foundation to begin with. The relationship God has predestined for you won't leave you broken and hurting. So pray and ask God to heal your heart and to strengthen you. Listen to sermons that uplift and enlighten you and Christian music that will lift your spirit during these times. Let God minister to you through His Word. *Never give up hope, and know that the next will be your best.*

I have allowed breakups to make me bitter in the past. I faced depression because of them and felt like my world was falling apart. I felt like I couldn't move forward with my life, and found myself becoming guarded and defensive, holding up walls to protect my heart. Eventually, I had to remind myself who my "daddy" is: Father God. I began to pray and listen to the Word of God, and I instantly felt myself feeling and getting better. After God healed my heart and helped me to release bitterness, I vowed never again to allow someone to come into my world and disturb my peace and put me back in a place of bitterness. Furthermore, rather than moping over a breakup, I learned to grow from it, learning to appreciate and embrace my own strength and ability to live outside of one. Trust me, you will survive. In fact, you will thrive. You will discover a strength you never thought you had and learn how to live an even happier life.

## NOTES

1.) Have you ever felt bitter after a experiencing a breakup?

2.) How did you overcome your bitterness?

# Day 12

## DOES AGE MATTER?

*Above all, be loving. This ties everything together perfectly.*
—Colossians 3:14

+ I will allow my heart to be my guide.

+ I will not put stipulations on love.

Age can be a major factor in a relationship. Age differences can be good and bad. In my opinion, age does not matter as long as both parties are of legal age, grown enough to make their own decisions. People mature at different rates, and everyone is raised differently. The way we're raised shapes our morals, and morals will always play a major part in our relationships. If you've been raised to respect yourself, you'll demand that your partner treat you right, respect your feelings, and be selfless. No two people are the same; therefore, people have different preferences when it comes to a mate, which is why you need to know yourself and know what you want. Be honest with your desires. If you're attracted to someone within a certain age bracket, that's your preference. It's your life, and you have to be comfortable with your decisions.

It's common to see young men with older women nowadays. Some younger men claim that the thing they like about older women is that they're easy and fun to talk to about certain things and that they're more financially stable. These women get a reputation and are often called "cougars" for certain reasons: they tend to be more experienced in the bedroom, and they usually know what a man wants—they know how to make a man feel like a king. Hey, I can't knock that. Many young men were raised by single mothers, grandmothers (or big mamas). Being raised by women, they know just what it takes to make a woman happy. They are more conscious of "the little things" that need to be taken care of that makes a woman feel special, such as pumping the gas, carrying the groceries, cooking for her, being respectful of her feelings, and spending quality time with her. These young guys were raised to be "old school," which is a good thing, trust me.

On the flip-side, you have those young ladies who enjoy dating older men. When asked why, one of the most common answers is that older men tend to be more financially stable, have more wisdom, they understand more life's many struggles, act more mature. Couple that with the fact that some of them are in excellent physical condition, not wasting their health because they're conscious of how precious good health is. Many younger women are looking for a man who is in a place in his life where he's done with playing games and is ready to treat a woman as his queen, and this tends to describe most older men.

Again, no two people are the same. Everyone wants what they for different reasons, so don't judge or look at them funny, and don't think of yourself as strange for having a certain preference. You don't know where a person is in life; just respect their decision as long as it's legal, and remember…when it comes to grown folks, age ain't nothing but a number.

## NOTES

1.) What age-range do you want your mate to be in?

2.) What age group are you more compatible with and why?

# Day 13

## DIFFERENCES IN OPINIONS

*But when completeness comes, what is in part disappears.*
—1 Corinthians 13:10.

• I will be open to making positive changes in my life.

• I will have more temperance.

You can always learn something new from your partner just as they can learn something new from you. In fact, one of the beautiful things about relationships is we constantly learn new things about our chosen partner, and this learning continues throughout our lives. In the beginning, differences can cause friction, but once we learn to stop criticizing our partner's differences and trying to make them more like us and we begin to respect their differences and even appreciate them, we'll begin to find balance and harmony in our relationships. We'll discover that what we call a difference in our mate might actually be a strength. We all have them: strengths and weaknesses. One person may be good at saving money while the other may be a spender. One may be a homebody, and the other may like to hang out. Your mate may want kids, but you might not want kids. One person may be soft-spoken, and the other might be loud. You've probably heard the old saying: "Opposites attract." Well, they do, and people come into our lives for a reason. People who are opposite of us come into our lives to add what we're lacking. For example, you may be a good financial saver, but a spender may come to teach you how to relax and enjoy life. And on the flipside, you're there to teach them how to be financially responsible and save for the future. The two of you balance each other out.

When it comes to differences such as lifestyle choices, having kids, and the likes, it's important to sit down together and have a good conversation about why you want what you want or don't want something. Understanding is the key. When understanding is present, this minimizes friction and establishes greater intimacy. Furthermore, when both of you are focused on serving one another and making each other happy, you'll be willing to reach a compromise.

Relationships bring out the best and the worst in us. Your partner is able to see things about you that may need to be changed in order to make you a better person, and vice-versa. No one can watch their own back and perform surgery on themselves, which is why it takes someone else to come and do for us what we can't do for ourselves. So don't be so quick to get defensive when your partner points out an area in your life where you may need to improve; that's one of the reasons God placed them in your life. However, the key is to avoid becoming impatient with your partner and yourself and expecting changes to occur overnight. Suppose you throw in the towel on the relationship too early. In that case, you may halt the process of growing and learning and delay the personal development the relationship is designed to produce inside of you. So don't let your feelings override your intelligence.

## NOTES

1.) How have you begun to prepare for the new season in your life?

_______________________________________________

_______________________________________________

# Day 14

## WHY IS HE/SHE
## SO DEFENSIVE?

*Trust in the Lord with all your heart and lean
not unto your own understanding.*
—Proverbs 3:5

+ I will have a voice in my relationship.

+ I will not make excuses for how people treat me.

When your mate is in defense-mode, this can make you question yourself: "What did I do?" "What did I say?" "Why is he/she upset with me?" "I only said…I only did…So I don't know why they're so angry." It may seem like your partner cringes each time you touch them. They might strike up an argument every time you try to talk and attempt to make you feel like the one who's wrong. They may question your credibility and even cause you to question your credibility…and sanity.

I learned that it's better to be slow to speak and quick to listen; that way, you can better understand your partner's perspective—know why they're upset, what their expectations are, why they feel the way they feel. There's always a reason behind someone's anger and disappointment; discovering that reason comes down to being a good listener. Rather than justifying your own actions, seek to see things from your partner's perspective. When you do this, you'll make your partner feel respected and honored; they'll feel as if you value their opinion and feelings. Peaceful resolutions, understanding, and showing love are always better than attacking one another and bumping heads, which only leads to defensiveness. So practice good listening skills, empathy, and patience, and you'll find your relationship moving in a positive direction.

54

## NOTES

1.) How do you respond to someone who seems to have lost or is losing respect for you?

_______________________________________________

_______________________________________________

_______________________________________________

_______________________________________________

_______________________________________________

_______________________________________________

_______________________________________________

_______________________________________________

_______________________________________________

# Day 15

## QUEEN STATUS

*Husbands love your wives, just as Christ loved
the church and gave himself up for her.*
—Ephesians 5:25

+ I deserve love.

+ I deserve respect.

As a woman, we must practice self-love before anyone else can love us. Never dumb-down and devalue yourself down for anyone. God wants us to be the best version of ourselves. The way we treat ourselves and take care of our kids and home will show our partners how to treat us. *What we allow others to do to us is what we choose to accept.* So if you're with someone who isn't treating you like the queen you are, it's because you allow it.

A high-status woman who highly values herself can be intimidating to an insecure man. But it is important for the fellas to know that women today are becoming more self-sufficient and aware of their value and worth; women today are earning their own money and taking care of themselves like never before. All of this has raised the bar even higher for many women, which is causing men to have to work that much harder to win a place in these women's lives. But don't feel like it is hopeless if you're not rich. For example, if a man does not make more money than his partner or he doesn't make a lot of money at all, then he must be able to excel in other ways and at other things. He should demonstrate his ability to manage the family finances well and be a good father figure to their kids (if they have any). It's not always about the money. Being faithful, spending quality time, being loyal, honest, and trustworthy are all factors that make a relationship work also.

# Day 16

## KING STATUS

*But you, man of God, flee from all this, and pursue righteousness, godliness, faith, love, endurance and gentleness.*
—1 Timothy 6:11

+ I am lovable.

+ I am worthy.

A man who carries himself as a king doesn't have to say much; his demeanor will speak for him. He projects confidence and knows what he wants in life. This type of man is admired by many, but only the right kind of woman will be able to gain access to him. *Men want to feel loved and appreciated, just like women, and only women who know how to love, honor, and respect a real man can handle one.*

Kings are respected because of how they carry themselves around others. A king will be a provider and a protector for his family; he will put their needs before his own. This type of man is a God-fearing man; he sets the tone for how the house will be run. Kings speak with wisdom and provide guidance to the household; they aren't afraid to take ownership over their mistakes, and they cover their families with prayer as priests of the home. Most importantly, a king knows how to respect his queen, affirming her and acknowledging her value. As the Bible says, he honors her as his equal; and he loves her the way Christ loves the church, putting her needs before his own and sacrificing his life for her. Only a queen can handle a king.

# Day 17

## STRIVING TO BE A
## PROVERBS 31 WOMAN

*She is clothed with strength and dignity.*
—Proverbs 31:25

+ I am a good woman.

+ I will seek God wholeheartedly.

The virtuous woman described by King Solomon in the Bible did not become a virtuous woman overnight. It takes time and discipline to become a virtuous woman.

One trait of a virtuous woman is she doesn't expose herself to any and everything. She carries herself with dignity and holds up a standard, thereby demanding respect. She doesn't entertain negativity because she knows the importance of protecting her ears and preserving her peace. This type of woman seeks God; she spends time in God's Word and spends time with God in prayer. This type of woman is focused on doing the will of God. She examines herself in the mirror and takes note of the areas in her life where she needs to improve, and she makes the necessary changes to become the best version of herself she can be. She is always improving upon herself. She loves and cherishes peace and love, and carries herself with respect while giving respect to others. She is valuable to others. That's a virtuous woman. That may sound like a tall order to fill, but understand that this is simply a standard to strive towards. She is the ideal woman, the symbol and mark of perfection by which we are able to judge our own actions and behaviors.

Be patient. The more you spend time with God and seek His

face, the more He transforms you into this incredible, unbelievable woman. You may feel like you're not growing, not changing into this type of woman at times. You may even feel like the opposite is happening: that you're falling to pieces. But don't worry. Again, it's all a part of the process. The God who began a great within you will complete it until the end.

# Day 18

## ARE YOU DATING
## TO ENTERTAIN?
### (Are you wasting your time?)

*Walk with the wise and become wise,*
*for a companion of fool's harm.*
—PROVERBS 13:20

• I do not want a "friends with benefits" arrangement with anyone.

• I refuse to be second best to anyone.

Dating for the wrong reason is dangerous; it can lead to heartache, pain, and dishonesty. When you jump into a relationship, both you and your partner should be open and honest about what your expectations are, and you should acknowledge the challenges and risks the two of you face as a result of being a couple. For example, if you are dating a coworker at your job, just know that things can go south, and if they do, you still have to face each other in the context of work. So you should have an agreement and understanding of the risk involved there.

Suppose you're dating someone that is in it for the wrong reason. In that case, chances are they'll engage in destructive behaviors such as cheating, remaining in communication with their ex, flirting with various other people, not investing time into you as they should, not acknowledging you around other people, not introducing you to their family and friends (keeping you a secret), and neglecting you. In essence, they are just wasting your time.

Don't settle for just anything just so that you can say, "I have someone—I'm in a relationship." You may find yourself compromising your standards and values and sacrificing your self-esteem just to make this claim, and nothing is worth losing these things. Know what you want and what you're not willing to put up with, and make sure your partner is serious about being in a relationship. If they're not serious, then you'll only be wasting your time while heading towards the inevitable heartbreak.

# Day 19

## ARE YOU DATING TO BUILD?
### (What are you building together?)

*Husbands love your wives, just as Christ loved
the church and gave himself up for her.*
—Ephesians 5:25

• I am ready for marriage.

• I am ready for stability in my life.

Building a relationship involves setting aside childishness, removing distractions, and making important changes in your life. To build a successful relationship, you must have respect for yourself and your partner; respect is foundational here. Remember: It takes two to make a relationship work, and both of you must want it to work.

It's important that you state your expectations upfront at the very beginning. Let your partner know what you're looking for and what you won't settle for. By doing this, you will avoid a lot of heartbreak and disappointment. When someone tells you they are not ready for a serious relationship, believe them! And don't be deceived into thinking you can convince them otherwise or you'll only end up hurt in the long run. As a young girl, I thought that I could keep a man in my life using my body, but as I got older, I realized that wasn't true. Once the initial attraction begins to fade, it takes other things to keep the relationship going: love, dedication, trust, respect, communication, and selflessness. People's needs extend beyond just the physical—beyond just sex. There are also mental, emotional, and spiritual needs that must be met. You have to think about everything you have to give and everything that is required to keep a functional relationship going.

I've discovered the importance of building a relationship using the right tools, the once mentioned above. Furthermore, I learned that it's important not to invest your heart into a relationship with a partner who's not interested in building a life together. Relationships are about commitment, not temporary thrills. Is your partner ready to build? Are they ready to grow alongside you? Are they willing to make sacrifices and changes for the sake of the relationship? Are they thinking about building a family together, or are they just trying to get over a specific hurdle in their life (looking for a rebound from a breakup, looking for sex, looking for some company due to loneliness, or they're unsure of what they're looking for, period)?

Remember: You don't date just to date; you date to determine whether or not the person you're with is a suitable partner in marriage, a life-partner, a soulmate. If your partner isn't thinking long-term, they're not ready to build anything with you.

---

---

---

---

---

---

# Day 20

## IN AND OUT

*The Rock! His work is perfect, for all His ways are just; A God of faithfulness and without injustice, Righteous and upright is he.*
—DEUTERONOMY 32:4

+ I do not want to play games.

+ I will set the bar for my life.

When a person isn't invested into a relationship, they'll have one foot in and one foot out of it. Again, if they're not fully invested into the relationship, you can't build together—there's no foundation to build upon. Again, one clear sign that your partner isn't fully invested in the relationship is they refuse to devote time to you. If your mate has time for other people, places, and things, this should be a red flag that he is not into you. There could either be a great deal of dishonesty or selfishness at play here. Either way, they're clearly communicating that they don't want you to be a critical part of his or her life.

Respect yourself enough not to let someone play with your heart and waste your time. If they don't want you, let them go. Never allow yourself to be someone's secret. Make sure that your mate is fully invested before even considering the possibility of marriage. *It is good to stay grounded like a tree whose roots are long.*

# Day 21

## ENCOURAGING ONE ANOTHER

*Therefore encourage one another and build each
other up, just as in fact you are doing.*
—1 Thessalonians 5:11

• I will speak life into my partner.

• I will encourage myself daily.

Compliments and encouragement in a relationship are necessary. Based on personal experience, I discovered that men like to be complimented and made to feel special. A compliment can be something as simple as telling your partner that you like the way they made you feel. Encourage your partner to run after their goals in life and be a better version of themselves for their own sake, not just for you. Compliment their characteristics and personality. Look for the good in them rather than the bad, and compliment them for the good you see in them. Compliments build confidence and strengthen the intimacy in your relationship. If you're not used to issuing out compliments to your partner, start practicing today. And a good place to start, by the way, is to start with yourself. Have you complimented yourself today? How you treat yourself is often indicative of how you'll treat those closest to you.

# Day 22

## HOW DO I SEE COMMITMENT?
### (What Are You Bringing?)

*For this is the message that you have heard from the
beginning, that we should love one another.*
—1 John 3:11

+ I will be the best version of myself.

+ I will be true to myself.

One question you should ask yourself is, "What will a person get when they receive me into his/her life?" I once heard Bishop T. D. Jakes say, "Everyone wants an asset; no one wants a liability." Which one are you: an asset or a liability? Do you add to another's life, or are you simply focused on draining what's inside of them through selfishness and unreasonable demands? Do you find yourself throwing out ultimatums if your partner doesn't do things your way or do what you want rather than engaging in compromise so that the two of you can be happy?

Look at your actions. Make sure you're an asset. Discover your value and worth and know what you're able to bring to the table. Realize that you MUST bring something to the table and not look for someone else to "make *you* happy". There are two people there: you and them. They have wants and needs too. They want to be happy also. Do you plan things for them, or do you simply wait for them to do all of the planning? Do you take the initiative, or do you always wait for them to make the first move?

Being in a committed relationship is tough; it takes work—lots of it. It's not for the faint of heart. It will test you in every way and bring out both the best and the worse in you. You're going to have to fight for your relationship, that is, if it's worth fighting for. But part of that fight entails you bringing 100%. You can't be lazy and act entitled. You have to be all in yourself and willing to do your part as well. Are you all in? Are you really doing *everything* you can on your part to make things work? Ask yourself that question.

_____________________________________________________

_____________________________________________________

_____________________________________________________

_____________________________________________________

_____________________________________________________

_____________________________________________________

_____________________________________________________

_____________________________________________________

# Day 23

## IS THE TIME STAMP FOR US
## OR THE WORLD?
### (Whose Deadline Is It?)

*But do not forget this one thing, dear friends: With the Lord a day is like a thousand years, and a thousand years are like a day.*
—2 Peter 3:8

◆ I will not rush the progress of my relationships.

◆ I will live by God's timetable rather than man's.

Everyone sets short-term and long-term goals for themselves in life. We all have deadlines (ex. "By the age of thirty, I want to be married" or "By the age of fifty, I want to be able to retire," etc.). Some of us want kids before a certain age or want to be engaged by a certain time. It is important to remember that God is the one with the master-plan for our lives. He has a timing and a season for certain things as it pertains us. That is why you shouldn't be in a rush for anything; instead, understanding that there is a time and there is a process to everything in our lives. And don't try to rush the process either.

You may want to live the ideal life, and you may feel you're ready for it—you're ready for the house with the white-picket-fence, the two kids, and a dog—but your partner isn't; this is the time to figure out whether or not it's worth the wait. Should you be patient and wait for your partner to become ready, or be willing to move on without them? In fact, God may be in the process of molding them. The question is, if you two are on different plains as far as maturity and goals are concerned, are you compatible? And if not, is it worth waiting? Is holding up your life for someone else a wise decision?

If the wait is worth it, however, then wait…and pray. Don't worry about what other people think either. Others will think you're investing too much time and hope in someone they think isn't good for you, but in your heart, you realize that love has no time-restraint or deadline. It takes time for important things to develop anyway. It takes time to mature, to build a relationship, to grow and develop. Sometimes, a diamond doesn't always appear to be a diamond; it may just look like a rock at first, so you don't want to be so quick to give up on someone who's really a diamond in the rough.

I know I've hit you with a lot to consider. But ask yourself whether or not you are moving based on God's time-line or yours? And when it comes to the relationship, know that it takes divine guidance and wisdom in this situation to know which route you should take. You may move too fast and end up losing a diamond in the rough or stay too long only to discover you've wasted valuable time on a dull rock.

________________________________________

________________________________________

________________________________________

________________________________________

________________________________________

# Day 24

## PROCEED WITH CAUTION
### (Read the Signs)

*Love is patient, love is kind. It does not*
*envy, it does not boast, it is not proud.*
—1 Corinthians 13:4

+ I will be still and wait on God.

+ I will not compromise just to accommodate my flesh.

I can't overstate the importance of observing red flags in a relationship. Even if a person isn't the maturest person, they can still be respectful and civil. However, when a person is abusive, it doesn't matter how much money they have, how old they are, or anything else; abuse is an indication that they're bad news and you don't need to be around them. Your intuition will pick up on red flags, so trust your gut in these matters. To overlook your intuition and dismiss a red flag is to open yourself up to abuses you don't need. Many people do this to themselves, and to justify accepting abusive and bad behavior from their partner, they make excuses for them: "Oh, he's just stressed," "I get on his nerves sometimes, but he doesn't mean to treat me that way," "She loves me, she just doesn't know how to control her temper when she gets angry or upset."

Red flags include bad behaviors such as physical and emotional abuse, lying, neglecting your partner for another person or something else, disrespecting and belittling your partner, and cheating, among other things. If your partner is engaging in these behaviors, address them immediately and let them know you won't remain with them if they continue to do these things. Sure, you can give them another chance, but you also need to think about your future. If they can't commit to making important changes for your sake and theirs, then you need to make the decision that's best for you in this situation. You need to way all of your options: counseling, separation, divorce, etc. I don't make it a point of telling people to leave their partners because every situation is different, but there are some things no one should live with and put up with. And if you marry someone who's already throwing up red flags in your face, you can expect more of that after the wedding, and you have to ask yourself if that's something you can see yourself living with for the rest of your life.

# Day 25

## PREDATORS OF THE HEART

*Do not be anxious about anything, but in every sit-
uation, by prater and petition, with thanks-
giving, present your requests to God.*
—Philippians 4:6

- I will not allow anxiety to overtake me.

- I will remain calm during the storms in my life.

Many things that can break our hearts, but the heartbreak a relationship brings is perhaps the worse; it feels like having your heart ripped out of your chest. Catching your spouse cheating, being lied to, being manipulated, misunderstood, beaten on, and disrespected are things more common to intimate relationships, and the people who do these things often have a history of preying on people who're in search of love.

I often reminisce over my life, thinking about moments when I found myself dealing with these kinds of things. I learned as a result of falling for relationship predators what to look for in a mate. I learned what to look out for, how to spot red flags, and how to pray for the right partner. As a result of being victimized, I learned how to build boundaries and value myself as an individual created in the image of God. Yeah, predators are out there, but you don't have to become prey if you do the things I'd just mentioned.

## Notes

1.) After experiencing a heartbreak, how did you overcome it and move forward with your life?

_______________________________________

_______________________________________

_______________________________________

_______________________________________

_______________________________________

_______________________________________

_______________________________________

_______________________________________

_______________________________________

# Day 26

## COPING WITH LONELINESS

*Be strong and courageous. Do not be afraid or terri-*
*fied because of them, for the Lord your God goes with*
*you, he will never leave you nor forsake you.*
*—Deuteronomy 31:6*

• I will spend more time with my family and friends.

• I will focus on healing.

Having a partner can make you feel complete as an individual. Having someone with you day in and day out is special. Being the first person they see when they open their eyes, and the last one they see before they go to bed is priceless. Having someone to share your heart with and every piece of exciting news with is awesome. But when a relationship ends, it can leave you feeling lost, confused, devastated, and lonely. You may get tempted to call or text your ex because of the memories that you have of them, but fight it. Like I said before, keep yourself busy with things like hobbies and other activities. Furthermore, don't isolate yourself; go out with friends and family. Defeat loneliness by reaching out to people and getting involved with activities that lead to new relationships.

Healing takes time, and it is not easy. We must allow ourselves to feel the pain. We must accept the new changes in our lives and ask God for the strength to move forward. Progress does not always feel good. Sometimes, we can get desperate and look for God to replace our exes right away (called "rebound") just to fill in a void in our souls, but that's not wise either. Just be patient and let the healing occur. Let God mold you into a better person so that you'll be ready once someone new comes along.

# Day 27

## HEAD OVER HEART DECISIONS

*The name of the Lord is a fortified tower;*
*the righteous run to it and are safe.*
—Proverbs 18:10

• I will put myself first.

• I will make wise decisions based on facts and not emotions.

When we invest our time and hearts into a person, it gets difficult to pull away from them. Also, the love that we have for them can becloud our judgement, making it difficult to make healthy decisions. But we must not allow our emotions to make the decisions for us. We must not! Again, think about the "why" in every situation: "Why did I leave in the first place? Why didn't things work? Is it worth going back to that?" When you focus on the "why" instead of how you feel, now you're thinking with your head and not your heart.

There have been times when I chose to follow my heart rather than my head out of fear of hurting the other person's feelings, but eventually, this led to me hurting myself more than anything. I had to realize that I also matter, and work to prioritize my feelings, peace, and future. In my case, I had to think about the example I was setting for my kids by remaining in a bad relationship. Once I did this, I discovered that I didn't need to apologize for my intuition and allow myself to be manipulated by my feelings. Your thoughts aren't wrong because they don't line up with someone else's perspective. Begin to practice godly discernment, which comes from His Holy Spirit. That will allow you to have insight (seeing things deeper), which is greater than physical eye-sight (seeing things on the surface).

# Day 28

## DOES YOUR LOVE GIVE LIGHT OR DARKNESS?

*Their hearts are secure, they will have no fear; in
the end they will look in triumph on their foes.*
—Psalm 112:8

+ I will be peaceful, loving, and nurturing.

+ I will not give off toxic energy.

Darkness is filled with negativity. Things like complaining and fault-finding characterize darkness, and it is associated with bitterness. Love, on the other hand, is beautiful. Love is patient and kind; it gives compliments and speaks life into your partner. Love is positive and has great energy. Most of all, love is filled with patience and wisdom.

During certain defining moments, our true character shows. Be slow how you react in different circumstances. Think before you act. Remain positive and hopeful and be careful not to burn a bridge simply because you're emotional at the moment. You never know if you'll need to cross that bridge again.

### Notes

1.) What do people get when they get you?

# Day 29

## LETTING GO OF RESENTMENT

*Don't sin by letting anger control you. Think
about it overnight and remain silent.*
—Psalm 4:4

• I will forgive.

• I will not hold negative things in my heart.

It is easy to become bitter when another person wrongs you. When wronged, we often look for answers, closure, and even revenge. People can do hurtful things to us, but know that God will always turn these situations around and make them work for your good when you trust Him rather than seeking revenge.

Bitterness can consume us with thoughts and memories of what was done to us, causing us to forget about the good things that have happened to us. I've been there. But the way I overcame the bitterness of a bad breakup was I reminded myself that was not my final chapter. God wrote the story of our lives out from beginning to end; this filled me with a sense that greater was coming. Whenever God removes someone or something out of our lives, He always replaces it with someone or something better.

## NOTES

1.) When dealing with the hurts from your past, how did you overcome the feeling of resentment?

# Day 30

## CAN I LOVE AGAIN
## AFTER A HEARTBREAK?

Break-ups do not feel good. Like I said before, they can leave you in a sunken place; this can cause you to close your heart to love and a new relationship. Heartbreak is like sitting your hand on a hot stove—once you feel that pain for the first time, you'll never want to get near a stove again.

The only way I survived my ordeal was I had to pray a lot. I listened to sermons by Christian ministers and began to work on myself, allowing myself to process the pain while improving who I was. I had to forgive myself and accept what happened, realizing I couldn't change the past. After I allowed my heart to get healed, I was ready and able to open up my heart again and receive new love. I had to avoid carrying old baggage into a new relationship.

There is love after a heartbreak. I declare that your next experience with love will be different because you will be different; you will have a new mindset. With this new mindset, you will know your worth, and you will know what you are looking for.

### NOTES

1.) Was it difficult to walk away from your old relationships?

2.) How did you embrace your newness?

# ABOUT THE AUTHOR

Ashley Davis is a mother of two daughters. She was born and raised in Thomaston, Georgia. She has since relocated to Macon, Georgia.

Ashley is a licensed insurance agent for a fortune 500 company and a medical assistant. She is also the owner of Davis Kingdom Shiners, LLC. She wears many hats. She endeavors to never become complacent, but to keep striving to become a better version of herself daily.

To contact the author, go to

AshleyDavis.asd@gmail.com
www.AshleyShantel.com
Facebook: Ashley Davis
Instagram: Ashleyd_Speaks
Twitter: AshleyD_Speaks

www.ingramcontent.com/pod-product-compliance
Lightning Source LLC
Chambersburg PA
CBHW071457030726
47593CB00003B/1039